Swallows

Christine Butterworth

MACMILLAN

It is April.

The days are getting warmer.

Here come the swallows.

They will stay all summer.

2

Swallows fly here all the way
from Africa.
They take many weeks to get here.
They find their way by
the sun and the stars.

3

Each year the swallows come back and
nest in the same place.
They look for an old shed or barn.
Some people call them barn swallows.

The swallows like to live
near water.
They can find a place to sleep
in the reeds.
They can find many insects to eat.

A swallow can catch insects
as it flies.
It turns fast on its wide wings.
Its short beak opens wide
to trap the insects.

These birds are catching insects.
Can you see the swallows?
They are the birds with
the long forked tails.

A swallow is in the air
for most of the day.
It can even drink as it flies.
The swallow flies low over the water and
scoops up water into its beak.

Now it is late in the summer.
The swallows eat more and
more insects.
They grow new feathers.
They need strong wings to fly
back to Africa.

Have you seen swallows sitting together
on wires like this?
They sit like this when
the days get colder.
They feel it is time to leave.

Swallows do not like it when
the cold winds blow.
They are too small to keep warm
in the ice and snow.
One day the swallows leave.
They fly thousands of miles to Africa.
This is called migrating.

There are many dangers for
the swallows when they are migrating.
Some birds will be shot by hunters.
Others may die in storms at sea.
Some are blown by the wind and
cannot find the way.

12

When the swallows get to Africa
they have to fly over
miles of jungle.
Some of them die there.
The birds that die are old or weak.

13

A lot of swallows do get safely
across the jungle.
At last they can rest.
They will be safe and warm.

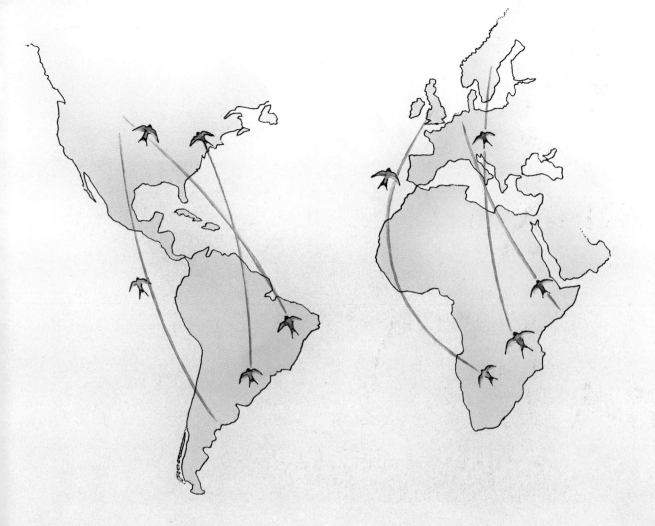

Here is a map.

Can you find our country on the map?

Can you see how the swallows

get from our country to Africa?

The swallows will stay in Africa
until it is spring again.
Then they will fly back to us.

When you see the swallows
arrive in the spring they are
thin and tired.
They need to rest.
They sit in the trees.
Then they find their old nests.

Look at these swallows.
They have come here from Africa.
They are looking for the nest
that they made last summer.
They will mend the nest and
use it again.

18

These two young swallows do not have
a nest of their own.
They have to look for a place
to make a new nest.

This barn is a good place.

The swallows fly inside.

They look for a shelf or a beam

where they can make a nest.

20

There is a pond near the barn.

The swallows fly out to the pond.

Each bird picks up a tiny bit

of mud in its beak.

The swallows use the mud
to make the nest.
They mix the mud with
hair and grass.
This makes the sides
of the nest very strong.

It takes the swallows a week
to make the nest.
When the nest is dry
it looks like a small bowl.
The swallows put soft grass and
feathers inside the nest.

Now the female bird lays her eggs.
They are white with brown spots.
They are as tiny as marbles.
How many eggs has she got?

The female swallow sits
on the eggs for two weeks.
She must keep the eggs warm or
they will not hatch.

When the eggs hatch
the baby birds come out.
Now the male and female swallows
are busy all day.

They catch insects to feed
the babies in the nest.
The baby swallows grow fast.
At three weeks old they
have grown their feathers.
They can start to fly.

Now the young swallows
are four weeks old.
They are as big as the parents.
The parents feed them as they fly.
The young swallows leave the nest
in the day but they sleep
in the nest at night.

After a while the young swallows
all leave the nest.
They sleep with other young swallows
in the barn or in the reeds
by the pond.

The parent birds get the nest ready
for more eggs.
They will have two more families
this summer.

The days are getting colder.
Summer is nearly over.
The young swallows are grown up now.
It is time for all the swallows
to fly back to Africa.

The swallows will spend
the winter in Africa where
they can be warm and well fed.